Table of Contents

Introduction...3

Tomato 3

Growing tomatoes in containers: 7 strategies for success......4

Just Follow This Steps To Complete Ur Garden.......................7

The Best Tomatoes For Containers 12

The advantages of container gardening.............................15

The Disadvantages Of Container Gardening 15

Common Mistakes Growing Tomatoes In Containers...........16

Soil in Containers Should Be a Good Mix 19

Adding Compost Or Garden Soil Can Be Beneficial...............21

Customize Your Mix To Suit Your Plants 21

My Recipe For Homemade Potting Soil..............................22

Make Your Own Soilless Mix 23

How to Water Container Gardens.....................................24

How Do I Ensure Good Drainage in Container Gardens? 26

How to Repot Container Plants 27

Choosing A Pot For A Plant..28

How To Plant In Pot Container Garden 29

Pest Problems...35

Container Plant Watering...36

How Often to Water Potted Plants 37

How Much Water for Container Plants 38

Tips for Watering Outdoor Potted Plants............................. 38

Conclusion 39

Introduction

Tomatoes are the most popular vegetable grown in gardens, but even small or no-space gardeners can enjoy a harvest of homegrown tomatoes when they plant in containers.Tomatoes are a vegetable that thrives when grown in pots and you can help ensure success when you pick the best varieties for containers and pair them with my seven strategies for growing a bumper crop of delicious tomatoes in pots.

There is no replacing the full rich flavor of a tomato that has been sun ripened in your own garden!

That wonderful deep rich sun kissed flavor will never be found in a tomato purchased from a supermarket.

The problem with growing tomatoes, that many of us face, is that we have become apartment dwellers with limited land space to plant a regular garden. All is not lost.

We can plant our tomatoes in a container, and quite successfully too. This page will show you several ways you too can have that wonderful taste of summer from tomatoes planted in containers on the patio, deck or balcony of your apartment.

Tomato

Tomatoes are fruits that are considered vegetables by nutritionists. Botanically, a fruit is a ripened flower ovary and contains seeds. Tomatoes, plums, zucchinis, and melons are all edible fruits, but things like maple "helicopters" and floating dandelion puffs are fruits too. For some reason, people got hung up on tomatoes, but the "fruit or vegetable" question could also work for any vegetable with seeds.

Now, nutritionally, the term "fruit" is used to describe sweet and fleshy botanical fruits, and "vegetable" is used to indicate a wide variety of plant parts that are not so high in fructose. In many cultures, vegetables tend to be served as part of the main dish or side, whereas sweet fruits are typically snacks or desserts. Thus, roots, tubers, stems, flower buds, leaves, and certain botanical fruits, including green beans, pumpkins, and of course tomatoes, are all considered vegetables by nutritionists. There is no hard-and-fast rule that clearly designates a botanical fruit as a vegetable, but, given that tomatoes are generally not used in desserts and are closely related to other fruit-vegetables (e.g., eggplants and peppers),it is not too counterintuitive for tomatoes to be classified as vegetables.

Growing tomatoes in containers: 7 strategies for success

1) Container selection

Match the pot size to the variety size. Some tomatoes, like 'Micro Tom' grow just a foot tall and can be planted in small, six-inch diameter containers. Others, like 'Sungold' can grow over seven-feet tall and need a large five to seven gallon container. When looking for the best tomatoes for containers, read the description of the variety noting its mature size and pick an appropriate-sized pot.

Once you've found the right sized pot, flip it over and check to see if it has drainage holes. Tomatoes need excellent drainage and if the pot has just a single drainage hole, you'll need to add more. This is easy to do with a drill if the pot is made from plastic or wood, harder if it's a ceramic pot. For that reason, I tend to grow my container tomatoes in plastic pots or fabric planters. Fabric pots are free-draining and don't need drainage holes. Many companies also offer planters with attached trellises for easy set-up and an instant tomato garden.

2) Growing medium

Tomatoes appreciate a well-drained soil but also grow best when given plenty of organic matter. To keep container-grown tomatoes happy, I fill my pots with a 50-50 mixture of a high-quality potting mix like Pro-Mix Vegetable and Herb and compost. Or, can just use a compost-rich planting medium like FoxFarm Ocean Forest Potting Soil.

3) Plant the seedlings deeply

Tomato plants have the lovely ability to form roots all along their stems. Planting the seedlings deeply encourages strong, deep-rooted plants. I bury the plants half deep in the potting mix, removing any leaves that would be under the soil.

4) Smart support

Super compact varieties like 'Red Robin' or cascading tomatoes for hanging baskets like 'Tumbler' don't require cages or stakes. Most other types do. For determinate or dwarf varieties that grow two to three feet tall, you can use tomato cages. For indeterminate, or vining tomatoes, which can grow six feet tall or more, you'll need to provide strong support for the vigorous plants. You can use heavy-duty, lifetime tomato cages, trellises, or stakes. As the plant grows, continue to tie the main stem loosely to the support every week or so. You can use twine or garden ties.

5) Plenty of sun

Tomatoes are sun-loving plants and produce the best harvest when placed in a spot with at least eight hours of light. If you have less light, avoid large-fruited tomatoes which need full sun to mature their fruits. Instead, plant cherry tomatoes which will still crop, although more modestly, when given 4 to 5 hours of daylight.

My Heartbreaker tomato plants grow about a foot tall and are the first to produce fruits in my garden. The pretty, heart-shaped tomatoes are sweet and perfect for salads.

6) Water

Consistent watering is essential when growing tomato plants in pots. Container-grown tomatoes are more prone to blossom end rot, a physiological disorder that results in a dark, leathery-looking spot to form on the blossom end of the fruit. Blossom end rot isn't caused by a disease but rather calcium deficiency typically from inconsistent watering. If you're allowing your tomato plants to wilt between waterings, you're more likely to see blossom end rot.

Watering frequency depends on the size of the plant, size of the pot, composition of the growing medium (compost helps hold water), weather, temperatures, and more. Some summer days I water my container tomatoes in the morning and afternoon. Sometimes it's just once a day or every two days. The soil should be slightly moist, but not wet. Stick a finger down into the potting mix and if it's dry an inch or two down, water.

Also be mindful that larger pots hold more soil volume and water. That means they need to be watered less often than small pots. Therefore, plant tomatoes in the largest pots you can. You can also buy or DIY self-watering planters which have reservoirs of water so that plants don't dry out between waterings.

7) Fertilize

Tomato plants are generally considered to be heavy feeders and require regular fertilization to produce a heavy crop of fruits. Many potting mixes come with a modest amount of fertilizer which is used up within the first few weeks. To ensure my plants have a steady supply of nutrients, I incorporate a slow-release organic tomato fertilizer into the soil when I fill the container. I also apply a liquid organic fertilizer every two to three weeks during the growing season.

Just Follow This Steps To Complete Ur Garden

1. Pick a Good Spot. Place pots where they'll receive at least six hours of sun. If pots aren't near a water source, make sure you can get a garden hose to them (or don't mind lugging a watering can around), because tomatoes

need steady moisture supply. Group pots together, but not so close that leaves rub against each other (that can help spread disease). Grouping pots helps shade the root zones of the plants in the inner pots, which can be helpful when plants are sitting on concrete or an asphalt driveway, both of which absorb and reflect heat.

2. Find the Best Tomatoes for You. Whether you want to grow tomatoes for snacking, cooking, sandwiches, slicing, or all the above, there are loads of varieties for you to choose from. Here are a few of our recommendations for tomatoes that grow well in pots.

- Bite-Sized
- Tumbling Tom Yellow Tomato (for hanging baskets)
- Husky Cherry Red Tomato
- Sweet Million Cherry Tomato
- Pastes & Sauces
- Roma Tomato
- Monica Roma Tomato
- Sunrise Sauce Tomato
- Slicing
- Bush Early Girl Tomato
- Better Bush Tomato
- Patio Tomato

3. Choose the Right Pot. Those seedlings may look small now, but a full-grown tomato plant needs a lot of space for a strong root system. For maximum production, the ideal pot size is 18-inch diameter for determinate tomatoes and 24-inch diameter for indeterminate

tomatoes. When using a fabric pot or other type sold by volume, aim for 20 gallons. It's fine to use a smaller container, like a 5-gallon bucket or 10-gallon container, but for best results, stick with the smaller patio- or bush-type tomatoes (such as Better Bush, Bush Goliath, or Patio). Know, too, that tomatoes in smaller pots require more watering and feeding. All containers (except fabric ones) need drainage holes, so be sure to drill several if none are present. If you live in a warm region like the Deep South, Texas, or Desert Southwest, you may want to avoid black plastic containers. They tend to hold a lot of heat, which warms the soil and can diminish plant growth.

4. Use Premium Quality Potting Soil. Garden soil from planting beds tends to be too heavy for containers — it will over-compact — and may contain disease organisms. Tomatoes are susceptible to diseases (such as blight) and pests (like nematodes) that can hang out in soil, and one advantage of growing in pots is that doing so can reduce outbreaks. Fill containers with premium quality potting mix, such as aged compost-enriched Miracle-Gro® Performance Organics®All Purpose Container Mix, for best results. Light and fluffy, it will provide plenty of space for air and moisture move through the soil.

5. Plant Tomatoes Properly. Be sure to dig a hole deep enough to cover two-thirds of the tomato stem to encourage more root growth. As a rule of thumb, wait to plant until after your area's last frost date. If a chilly night threatens, cover pots with a frost blanket and

swaddle them with blankets, straw, or burlap for extra protection.

6. Add Support. Insert a support when you plant each tomato, as doing so later on may disturb the growing roots. A traditional tomato cage or stake works well for determinate types. Use a string trellis, tall stake, tomato toutour, or sturdy cage for indeterminate tomatoes. To create your own tomato cages, bend metal fencing or hog wire into a cylindrical shape, then use wire to connect the ends. Insert it into the soil or slip it over the outside of the pot, then secure it to stakes driven firmly into the soil.

7. Cover the Soil. When planting tomatoes in pots, keep the soil at least one inch below the pot rim, so you can add a layer of mulch to help keep soil moist. You can use traditional mulch materials, like straw, shredded bark, chopped leaves, or newspaper (minus the glossy circulars). Paper decomposes quickly, especially in hottest regions, so plan to refresh the layer as needed during the growing season.

8. Water Regularly. Proper watering is a big key to success for growing tomatoes in pots. Keep soil consistently moist, but not saturated. (Inconsistent moisture can pave the way to blossom end rot.) Use the finger test to see if a plant needs water: If the top inch of soil is dry when you push your finger into it, it's time to give it a drink. (Plants larger than knee-high can require almost daily watering once summer heat arrives.) Place a saucer beneath each pot to catch water that runs through the soil, so plants can absorb that extra

moisture over the course of a hot day. (It will also protect decks and patios.) A drip irrigation system can help reduce the time you spend holding the hose, and will pay for itself quickly if you're raising a large crop of potted tomatoes. If you're only tending a few pots, time spent watering provides an opportunity to inspect plants and keep an eye out for problems. When summer vacation beckons, line up someone to do the watering if you hope to still have tomatoes to pick upon your return.

9. Feed Your Plants. While starting with premium potting mix will give your tomato plants a nutritious start, for best growth, you'll want to continue to feed them regularly throughout the growing season. Fertilize them with a continuous-release fertilizer like Miracle-Gro® Performance Organics® Edibles Plant Nutrition Granules. It will not only help your plants grow strong and produce lots of juicy tomatoes, but it contains calcium to help protect them against blossom end rot, too. As with all fertilizers, follow package instructions.

10. Clean Up at Season's End. Remove spent tomato plants from the pots at the end of the growing season. If you plan to use the same pots to grow anything in the tomato family (think tomatoes peppers, eggplants, potatoes) during the following season, you'll want to start with fresh soil. Discard any remaining soil, wash and scrub soil from pots, then sterilize them by wiping or spraying with a solution of one part bleach to 10 parts water.

The Best Tomatoes For Containers

Flip through any seed catalog and you'll quickly discover that there are a lot of varieties available to gardeners. And while any variety can be grown in a container if given the right-sized pot, support, and care, certain varieties really are the best tomatoes for containers.

The best tomatoes for containers: cherry tomatoes

Terenzo F1 – I've been growing this compact red cherry tomato for almost a decade. The plants are low-growing only reaching a height of about 18-inches, but they also trail, making this a great choice for hanging baskets and planters. I also like to tuck the plants along the edges of my raised beds where they cascade over the sides, and provide us with months of sweet fruits. Terenzo is an All-America Selections winner, lauded for its easy cultivation and large crop of delicious tomatoes.

Tumbler – Like Terenzo, Tumbler is a variety that is perfect for pots and baskets. Plant three seedlings in a 12-inch hanging basket and you'll be enjoying a bumper crop of one to two-inch diameter fruits all summer long.

Micro Tom – Perhaps the smallest of all tomato varieties, Micro Tom grows just six inches tall. It can be planted in a four to six-inch pot where it will produce several dozen fruits. The small red tomatoes are mildly sweet and average about a half inch across.

Tidy Treats – This is one of the best cherry tomatoes for containers! The plants are super vigorous but grow to a manageable four-feet tall. It's early to fruit, with the harvest beginning just eight weeks from transplanting. And the crop of sweet, red, one-inch diameter fruits are produced in abundance. Bet you can't eat just one! Support the plant with a strong tomato cage.

Sungold – My all-time favorite tomato, Sungold is an extremely popular variety for home gardens. It can also be grown in containers but because the plants are large, up to seven feet tall, the pots should be at least sixteen to eighteen inches across. The plants need to be supported with a strong trellis or tall stakes. Expect a generous harvest of incredibly sweet orange cherry tomatoes.

Heartbreaker – Part of a series of super dwarf varieties, Heartbreaker is perfect for hanging baskets or containers. The plants grow just a foot tall but mine consistently produce 40-50 tomatoes over the course of the summer. The fruits are, as the name implies, heart-shaped and quite sweet. The fruits are more cocktail-sized than cherry with most around one and a half inches in diameter.

The best tomatoes for containers: saladette & paste tomatoes

Glacier – Saladette tomatoes have small to medium-sized fruits which are typically early to mature. Glacier is a compact indeterminate Saladette variety that grows just three to four feet tall. The medium-small red fruits are borne in trusses and have a wonderful flavor.

Sunrise Sauce – A 2020 introduction, Sunrise Sauce is a paste tomato that grows just 30 to 36 inches tall, making it an excellent choice for pots. Use a tomato cage to provide support.

Called 'the perfect patio tomato' by Johnny's Selected Seeds, this productive cultivar bears 4 to 6 ounce fruits that are round to oval and bright gold in color. The fruits are produced over a short period of time which is ideal for anyone wishing to make tomato sauce.

Plum Regal – Another bush-type paste tomato, Plum Regal is popular for its disease resistance which also includes resistance to late blight. The plants grow three to four feet tall and produce 4 ounce, plum-shaped fruits that are deep red in color.

The best tomatoes for containers: large-fruited tomatoes

Tasmanian Chocolate – Tasmanian Chocolate is one of the open-pollinated varieties produced by the Dwarf Tomato Project. The goal of the project was to introduce tomatoes that offered heirloom flavor on compact plants and this is a standout variety that is perfect for pots.   The mature plants grow just three-feet tall yet produce a good harvest of 6 ounce, burgundy fruits with a sublime, rich flavor.   Defiant PhR – If you're looking for a disease-resistant slicing tomatoes that also tastes great, look no further than Defiant PhR. It boasts high resistance to late blight, Fusarium wilt, and Verticillium wilt. The determinate, container-friendly plants grow about four-feet tall and begin to produce their bounty of 6 to 8 ounce fruits just 65 days after transplanting.

Galahad – An All-America Selections winning variety, Galahad offers many outstanding characteristics. The compact, four-foot tall plants are resistance to common tomato diseases like Fusarium wilt, late blight, gray leaf spot, and tomato spotted wilt virus. They also yield dozens of medium-large 7 to 12 ounce fruits that have a meaty texture and sweet flavor.

The advantages of container gardening

- Containers can be sited close to the classroom, reducing problems of supervision
- They are small and maneagable so children can care for them easily and even take them home for the holidays
- Smaller containers can be started indoors and transferred outside when the weather improves
- Containers that are accessible for everyone can be used
- Growing in containers enables you to grow plants that are unsuitable for your school soil, such as blueberries that need ericaceous (acid) soil
- Containers can brighten up an area or be used to disguise 'eyesores'
- There is less chance of pest damage in containers

The Disadvantages Of Container Gardening

- Containers can dry out easily so need watering and feeding more frequently
- They are easy for intruders to steal
- Only small amounts of vegetables can be grown in containers, so match the size of the crop to the container
- Pots can restrict plant growth. This can also be an advantage making some plants a more manageable size

Common Mistakes Growing Tomatoes In Containers

Growing tomatoes in containers is almost always an adventure. It can be incredibly rewarding, or flat out disastrous – sometimes for reasons beyond your control. But there are some common mistakes (trust me, I've made most of them, often more than once) that if you avoid them, will increase your chances of growing tomatoes in containers successfully.

Small Containers:

When it comes to tomato containers, bigger is better. The bigger your container, the more soil it will hold. The more soil you have the better the moisture retention and the more available nutrition will be to your plants – both of which are critical to happy, healthy tomato plants, and large harvests.

Too Much Water:

Watering your tomato plants properly is probably the main key to tomato success. Too much water and the plants drown, too little and you get blossom end rot. Inconsistent watering will get you blossom end rot, split tomatoes and stressed plants. You want to keep the soil in your pots consistently moist – not wet, but damp. Before you water, check if your soil is already moist. To do this put your finger into the soil about an inch. Water if the soil feels dry to the touch. Don't forget drainage too. Make sure your pot has large holes in the bottom so excess water can drain out. Pot feet are also a good idea if you have your pot on a patio or non-porous surface. Another great way to control water to your containers is to use a grow box. I've had great success with Earthbox and The Grow Box brands. For more info on keeping plants from drowning.

Too Little Water:

The amount of water your tomato plant needs will depend on heat, humidity, the size of your pot and the kind of potting soil you use. By mid-season, a large tomato plant may need watering at least once a day – sometimes twice. Also, when you water, make sure to really soak your plants – if you just give them a sip, the water will only wet the top layer of soil. Water until you see it coming out of the bottom of your pot. When you water, try to water the soil directly, not the leaves, because wet leaves can lead to fungus.

Don't bother with water crystals they are expensive and tests have shown that they aren't particularly effective. Overcrowding:

Putting lots of plants in one pot may seem like a good idea, but it usually is counterproductive. Unless my pot is tremendous (more like a raised bed) I only put one tomato plant per pot. To get an idea of minimum size, I have successfully grown one huge tomato plant in large reusable grocery bag and that's about as small as I'd go per plant.

Not Enough Sun:

Tomatoes are sun lovers and need full sun – which means that they need unobstructed, direct sunlight for 6-8 hours a day – no cheating or skimping. Many people (myself included) chronically overestimate how much sun an area gets. Really figure this out

– either with a watch or a sunlight meter – before you plant up your pots.

Chilly Tomatoes:

Along with sun, tomatoes like warm temperatures. While it might feel like you're getting a jump on the season by putting your tomatoes out early, they will not really do anything until it is consistently warm. If you do want to get a jump on the season, you can either cover your tomatoes with cloches, or plastic when it's cold, or do what I generally do which is to put them on carts and wagons and haul them in and out of my garage until temperatures warm up. Also, don't forget to harden off your seedlings.

Starving your plants:

Tomatoes are heavy feeders and need to be fertilized, if you aren't using a pre-fertilized potting soil. Most potting mixes has very few of the nutrients that your plants require to grow and be healthy so you will need to add those nutrients to the soil, or stimulate the ones already there, if your mix is heavy on compost. There are many fertilizers to choose from but I use either an all-purpose organic slow-release fertilizer, or one designed especially for growing tomatoes or vegetables, which I mix into my potting soil. In addition, I use a diluted fish emulsion/seaweed liquid, once every week or two.

Choosing the Wrong Variety of Tomato:

I disagree with conventional the wisdom here that suggests tomatoes with "patio," in their name. I think that most patio tomatoes taste, well, more like patio pavers than tomatoes. I love growing huge luscious tomatoes and sprawling cherry tomatoes. To me tomatoes are all about taste and texture and I don't want to bother growing them if they aren't totally delicious. Here are some of my favorite tomato varieties.

Growing Tomatoes Upside-Down:

A lot of people swear by growing tomatoes upside-down. Not me. I have tried it several ways and haven't found any to be all that great. I see the point of growing tomatoes that hang – just not upside down. If you want to know why, here's an article on the Upsides and Downsides of Upside-Down Tomatoes.

Staking or Caging too Late:

This is one of my chronic mistakes. I always forget how fast tomatoes grow and don't stake or cage them until they are huge and unwieldy. It is much better to set up your cages or stakes before your tomatoes get too big. Here is a video on how to build a bamboo tomato cage .

Soil in Containers Should Be a Good Mix

I work hard to ensure that the soil in my garden is the best I can give my plants, and they reward me with robust health. Yet that same good soil if transferred to a container would cause the plants in it to languish. That's because garden soil doesn't offer enough air, water, or nutrients to a plant growing in a container. Potting soils are specifically formulated to overcome these limitations.

One of the most important things a potting soil needs to do is provide roots access to air by letting water drain away from them. In the ground, the soil is usually deep enough to let excess water drain beyond root zones. In pots, however, water tends to accumulate at the bottom, despite drainage holes. The smaller the pore spaces of the soil in the pot, the higher that water layer will reach. Larger pores, formed by adding mineral aggregates to potting soils, readily admit water into the soil, then carry it through the medium and out the bottom. Then, all those large, empty spaces can fill with air.

Perlite, vermiculite, calcined clay (kitty litter), and sand are the mineral aggregates most commonly used in potting soils. Perlite and vermiculite are lightweight volcanic rocks naturally filled with air. I prefer perlite over the others because it does not decompose with time nor lose its aerating ability if the potting mix is compressed. Vermiculite is a valuable additive because it prevents some nutrients from leaching away, and it even provides a bit of potassium and magnesium.

A potting mix also must have ingredients that help it retain moisture. This is where organic materials—usually peat moss, sphagnum moss, or coir—come in. They cling to some of the water that the aggregates are helping to drain. Organic materials also hold on to nutrients that might otherwise wash away.

In addition to peat moss, vermiculite, and perlite, commercial mixes often contain sawdust or various grades of shredded bark. Lime may be added to help balance the acidity of the peat moss, and a small dose of fertilizer can often make up for the lack of nutrients.

Adding Compost Or Garden Soil Can Be Beneficial

Most gardeners make potting soil by combining perlite or vemiculite with peat or sphagnum moss. Two other organic materials that you could add to your potting mix are leaf mold and compost, which offer a wide spectrum of nutrients.

Adding some garden soil to a homemade potting mix contributes bulk while buffering against pH changes and nutrient deficiencies. The reason that garden soil is rarely added to commercial mixes is because of the difficulty in obtaining a steady supply that is consistent in quality and free of toxins such as herbicide residues.

Customize Your Mix To Suit Your Plants

Whether you use a manufactured or homemade potting mix, it's a good idea to have extra mineral aggregate and organic materials on hand to suit some plants' special needs. I add extra aggregate for plants that like their soil on the dry side. I add extra peat moss to my mixes for plants that prefer constantly moist soils. I grow top-heavy plants in a mix amended with calcined clay or sand to add weight to the pot.

Soilless potting mixes are relatively free of living organisms, but mixes made with soil or compost are not. Some gardeners talk about "sterilizing" their potting mixes by baking them in the oven to rid the soil of harmful organisms, limiting the hazards of damping-off and other diseases. What I hope they mean is that they "pasteurize" their mixes. Heating homemade potting mixes to sterilizing temperatures wipes out all living things, beneficial and detrimental, leaving a clean slate for possible invasion of pathogens and causing nutritional problems such as ammonia toxicity. Pasteurization, which occurs at lower temperatures, kills only a fraction of the organisms. The best way to pasteurize your soil is to put it in a baking pan with a potato embedded in the soil. Bake it at 350°F for about 45 minutes. When the potato is cooked, the potting mix is ready.

I don't pasteurize my potting mix. I rely, instead, on healthy container-gardening practices such as timely watering, good air circulation, and adequate light to avoid disease problems. Beneficial microorganisms in compost and garden soil also help fend off pests.

My Recipe For Homemade Potting Soil

I've found that making my own potting soil produces better results than commercial mixes and eliminates the need to monitor my containers' nutrient and pH levels. With plenty of good soil in my backyard, I have no trouble making this traditional potting medium. It features a mixed bag of ingredients, but I figure that plants, like humans, benefit from a varied diet. This mix can support plants for a year or two without additional fertilization.

Mix 2 gallons each of:

- Peat moss
- Perlite
- Compost

- Garden soil

with 1/2 cup each of:

- Dolomitic limestone
- Soybean meal
- Greensand
- Rock phosphate
- Kelp powder

I place a 1/2-inch mesh screen over my garden cart and sift the peat moss, compost, and garden soil to remove any large particles. I then add the remaining ingredients and turn the materials over repeatedly with a shovel, adding water if the mix seems dry. After a few incantations, the stuff is ready to work its magic on everything from my tomato seedlings to my weeping fig.

Make Your Own Soilless Mix

Years ago, Cornell University scientists came up with a formula for a soilless potting mix, which forms the basis for many commercial potting mixes on the market today. By following this recipe, you can easily replicate what is sold in bags at the garden center.

Ingredients

- 1 bushel peat moss
- 1 bushel perlite or vermiculite
- 1/2 pound dolomitic limestone
- 1 pound 5-10-5 fertilizer

- 1 1/2 ounces 20% superphosphate fertilizer

Mix the ingredients thoroughly. The mix is initially hard to wet, so moisten it as you stir it. This saves the trouble of doing so each time you remove some for use.

How to Water Container Gardens

Give outdoor living spaces pizzazz with pots, window boxes and hanging baskets. Bright and perky container gardens dress a home with living color that's tough to beat. The secret to keeping container gardens looking their best hinges on one activity: watering. Water too much or too little, and your pots will quickly become eyesores.

How do you know when to water? If plants wilt, that's usually a sign soil is dry, but plants succumbing to root rot also wilt, so you need to check soil to know if it's dry. Double-check by looking at soil (dry soil is lighter colored) or slipping a finger into pots. Another way to check for soil dryness is to gently lift the edge of a pot. Dry pots weigh less (lift one just after watering to learn how it feels when wet).

At the start of the growing season, plants need to be watered less frequently. As summer heat starts to sizzle and plants become lush, you may be watering containers once or even twice daily. Larger pots need watering less often than smaller ones, so it pays to embrace a bigger-is-better theme when it comes to containers.

Commercial bagged potting mixes designed for use in containers give the best results in terms of plant growth. These are soilless mixes, using a blend of various materials, including ground bark, coir, peat moss and perlite. Container blends don't get waterlogged easily, which also means they need to be watered more frequently.

You can improve the way that commercial container mixes retain moisture in several ways. Blend water absorbing crystals into soil. These crystals turn into gel as they absorb water and slowly release it to plant roots. Or try using water-absorbent mats in the base of pots. These mats absorb and retain moisture, making it available to plant roots over the course of several days.

You'll find several different types of water-absorbent mats. Hydromats are usually made from slow-to-biodegrade materials and offer variable degrees of longevity and reusability. Coir mats, sometimes sold as coco mats, biodegrade eventually. Hydromats made from polyethylene batting (similar to quilt batting) are washable and reusable from year to year, offering sustainability.

Self-watering conversion kits transform any container into a self-watering pot, or you can skip the kit and simply buy self-watering pots. These pots contain a reservoir in the bottom for holding water that keeps soil moist.

Drip irrigation systems for containers can make watering a hands-free affair. Install traditional microtubing systems that supply water via a hose and timer, or slip an inverted water-filled container, like a bottle of some type, into soil. Water moves or drips into soil as needed.

Many gardeners grab watering cans to irrigate pots or outfit a hose with a watering wand. Invest in a high-quality wand that allows you to buy replacement parts. That saves you money over the long haul, so that instead of replacing a wand each year, you might only need to replace the nozzle or turn-off valve every few years.

How Do I Ensure Good Drainage in Container Gardens?

This is a common piece of gardening advice, but it's true only for pots that don't have holes. If you're placing a container plant inside a larger, hole-less container, putting coarse material in the bottom of the outer container helps keep the plant's roots out of excess water. But if you're planting directly in the larger container, having gravel in the bottom is only a partial help to ensuring your plant's roots don't rot.

But the key point to remember: gravel in the bottom of a pot with holes does absolutely no good in ensuring good drainage. That's because water naturally flows toward finer material, not away from it, so the large air spaces between the pieces of gravel don't "pull" the water into them. So, at most, the gravel or clay shards simply prevent bits of soil from exiting through the holes.

The best way to ensure good drainage is to use a good-quality potting soil. Never use garden soil, because it's too dense for potting.

How to Repot Container Plants

Most healthy container garden plants eventually outgrow their pots. A good way to reinvigorate a rootbound plant is to repot it. In my former job as a greenhouse manager, I spent a lot of time repotting container plants.

Recognizing when it's time to repot is the first step. Telltale signs include soil that dries out quickly or has become degraded; roots tightly packed within a pot or protruding from drainage holes; and water sitting on the soil surface too long after watering. Often a plant simply looks top-heavy or as if it might burst out of its pot. The best time to repot most plants is when they're actively growing, in the spring or summer. However, plants can usually handle repotting whenever the situation warrants it.

A plant ready for repotting should slide out with the soil in one piece. If much of the soil falls free of the roots, the plant may not need repotting. If it does, there will likely be a solid soil-and-root mass in the shape of the just-removed pot. Roots should be white or light-colored. Black, dark-colored, or foul-smelling roots are usually signs of a serious problem, such as fungal disease.The second step is to get a plant out of its pot. If a plant is rootbound, it helps to water the root ball thoroughly in advance. For plants in small to medium pots, invert the pot and support the top of the root ball with one hand. Put your other hand on the bottom of the pot and use a downward throwing motion with an abrupt stop. Many plants will slip out after one or two throws. If not, knock the edge of the pot against a sturdy surface, such as a potting bench, still holding the pot with both hands. It may take a few good whacks to release the plant; be careful not to break the pot.

Roots packed tightly in a pot don't take up nutrients efficiently. To promote good nutrient absorption, trim the roots and loosen up the root ball before replanting. Use a sharp knife or pruning shears for this job, removing as much as the bottom third of the root ball if necessary. Don't be surprised if what you cut off is a thick tangle of root tissue. Also make three or four vertical cuts about a third of the way up the remaining root ball.

Cut through any roots growing in a circular pattern to help prevent the plant from strangling itself with its own roots as it grows. If the roots are thick along the sides of the root ball, shave or peel away the outer layer. Or gently untangle the root ball with your fingers as if you were mussing someone's hair. Do this along the top edge of the root ball, too.

The proper size of the new pot depends on the plant and its potential growth rate, how well it's growing under current conditions, and the ultimate size desired for the plant. Rely on your own idea of what a healthy specimen of a particular species should look like. When in doubt, go with a pot the next size up.

Choosing A Pot For A Plant

Choose a pot slightly bigger than the root ball.

To keep soil from leaking out the bottom of the pot, cover its drainage hole(s) with a paper towel, coffee filter, mesh screen, or pot shard. If you use a pot shard, place it convex side up to avoid sealing the hole. While it's common practice to put gravel or charcoal in the bottom of pots, they don't help with drainage and take up valuable space, so I don't recommend using them.

To repot a small plant that's easy to lift, put a few inches of moist soil in the pot and tamp it down lightly. Place the plant in the pot, centering it. The goal is to get the top of the root ball to sit about an inch below the rim of the pot. If the plant is in too deep, gently raise it and add more soil. If it sits too high, remove the plant and dig out some soil, or just dump the soil out and start over.

Now, fill the space around the root ball with soil. I've noticed that there are two approaches to this job — "stuffing" and "filling." Stuffers like to press soil in around a plant. Fillers like to fill the pot to the brim and let the soil settle in during the first few waterings. I'm usually a filler, but I do stuff a bit at times, especially with top-heavy plants that need to be steadied. Whether you stuff or fill, leave some room at the top so the pot can hold enough water with each watering to thoroughly moisten the soil.

How To Plant In Pot Container Garden

What a Plant Wants

After you've thought about what you want, consider what you can provide the plants given your environment, space and time commitment. Of course, plants need light, food, air and water, but the quality and quantity varies from plant to plant.

Space

Find out how big your plants will be when mature and make sure your container can accommodate that. Dwarf varieties usually do well in containers since they are small by nature.

Potting Mix

Container plants do best in a potting mix rather than in garden soil which can compact easily. Often garden soil contains weed seeds, pests and other critters you don't want in your containers.

Look for a mix that is light, fluffy, drains well and contains enough organic material to hold water and nutrients. You can purchase a pre-mixed potting soil or make your own.

When purchasing potting soil (not really soil at all) read the package carefully. Instead of buying something labeled "topsoil" or "compost" which could be made of just about anything, invest in high quality organic potting soil.

If you choose to make your own, find a good recipe and experiment. A classic soil-based mix is:

- 1 part peat moss or mature compost
- 1 part garden loam or topsoil
- 1 part clean builder's sand or perlite

Water

Watering plants in containers is different than watering plants directly in the soil. Potting soil is often less dense than garden soil and thus holds less water. Additionally, the pot restricts the amount of soil to hold water. And because the pots are above ground, they don't have all that mass around them to keep cool.

Too much or too little water will kill your plants. The idea is to keep the soil moist throughout, but not wet. Many container-grown plants need to be watered once or twice a day when it is hot.

Use a watering can or garden hose to wet the soil directly (not just the leaves!). If you still can't tell how much water is needed, consider a digital moisture meter for an exact reading.

If you plan to be away from home for several days a drip irrigation system can keep your plants happy. Purchase one or make your own.

You can also retain water longer by adding "agro-polymers" (sold under the name Soil Moist) to the soil or potting mix before you plant.

Mulch

Adding organic mulch to the top of your containers will retain moisture on warm days and add nutrients to the soil (remember that nutrients leach out each time you water and need to be replaced.)

Sunlight

Most plants need 7-12 hours of sunlight a day (especially herbs and vegetables with fruits). If you don't have that, look for shade tolerating varieties like spinach and chard.

Full Sun: Between 6 and 8 hours of direct sunlight per day.

Partial Sun: Plants require between 4 and 6 hours of sunlight a day, preferably in the morning and early afternoon.

Shade: Less than 4 hours of direct sunlight per day, with filtered sunlight during the rest of the day.

When you move your containers indoors for the winter, you may need to give them an extra sunlight-boost with plant grow lights. These specially designed lights simulate the sun and help plants thrive through the dark of winter.

Temperature

Plants grow best at temperatures between 55 and 75° F. Without the insulating earth around them, the roots of container plants get hotter and colder more quickly than their in-ground counterparts.

Move containers inside before it frosts. Provide shade (consider grouping pots together to shade each other) when it gets too hot. Some folks "plant" their containers part way in the ground for insulation.

Nutrients/ Fertilizers

Nutrient solutions such as compost teas, worm teas made from worm castings, as well as liquid organic fertilizers, fish emulsion and kelp meal provide needed nitrogen, phosphorous and potassium in addition to micronutrients and organic compounds.

Better than synthetic fertilizers, these organic fertilizers won't burn your plants and supply the necessary macronutrients as well as many micronutrients, minerals, amino acids and vitamins. Most release their nutrients slowly — a good watering gets them started — giving you long-lasting, healthy results. At Planet Natural, we carry a variety of organic formulas — including guanos — designed to encourage growth, blooms and bountiful harvests.

Alaska MorBloom

Derived from Atlantic fish, phosphoric acid and potash, Alaska MorBloom stimulates exceptional budding and blooming on all flowering plants. Brightens colors in flowers and foliage and promotes vigorous root growth, too! Mix 1-3 Tbsp per gallon of water to encourage budding in flowers, vegetables and ornamental houseplants.

Timing is everything when fertilizing as plant nutrient needs change as the plant grows. Annual plants, for example, benefit most when fertilized with a solution high in nitrogen when they are first planted (for growth and leaf development) and then switched to a low-nitrogen, high-phosphorus solution to encourage blooming.

Since nutrients leach from the soil every time your container plants are watered, it is important to add fertilizer every week or two.

Time

You'll need to devote some time most days to your containers. Between watering, pruning, dead heading and harvesting your crops, container gardens need your devotion.

Planting

When it is time to put your plants in their pots, follow these simple directions.

Wash your pot or container with warm, soapy water. Rinse well.

Dampen the potting mix — either in the bag (if you bought it) or in the container you mixed it in.

Partially fill the container with the prepared potting mix. If your container is large and/or heavy, fill it at the location where it will live. (Do not add pot shards or gravel to the bottom of the container, this will actually decrease drainage.)

Gently remove the plant from its original container. If it is rootbound, loosen the roots before planting (see Salvaging Rootbound Plants).

Set the plant in the new pot at the same depth as the old container and 1 to 2 inches below the rim of the pot.

Add soil to the container and pack it gently around the plant.

Water thoroughly with kelp extract or a compost tea to help it adjust to its new home.

Add Spanish moss or mulch to the top to help retain water.

Pest Problems

Container plants often suffer less pest attacks because they live in a cleaner and more frequently inspected environment than garden or yard plants. However, that doesn't make them immune from insects, diseases or other problems. Insects can creep into any garden and fungal spores are present in the air at all times.

Einstein Oil

All ingredients are 100% non-toxic and will keep leaves clean and plants healthy.

A popular leaf shine and houseplant cleaner, Einstein Oil contains the finest quality, first extraction, cold-pressed neem oil. It is also enhanced with several other potent herbal ingredients to keep leaves clean and plants healthy. All ingredients are 100% non-toxic and the best available.

- First off, try to avoid pests.
- Inspect plants before purchasing them to make sure they are healthy. Then gently wash them before planting.
- Use clean potting mix and clean containers.
- Wash your hands and tools, too.
- Make sure you are growing plants in the best conditions.
- Get rid of plants that are already infested and have lost more than half of their leaves.
- If, after all that, you still have a pest situation try Integrated Pest Management (IPM).

Monitor for pests daily when you water. Don't forget to look on the underside of leaves — it's a great hideout for hungry bugs or their eggs. Figure out what pest you are dealing with. If you aren't sure ask your local extension service. This way you can choose pest control methods specific to your problem, rather than pouring different chemicals on the plant while trying to figure out what works. Decide how much you are willing to deal with. The idea is to control the pest, not eradicate it. Can you live with the edges of a few leaves munched? How about your tomatoes chewed up?

If you need to take action use safe pest control measures that are least harmful to you, your plants, and the environment.

Problems with smaller pests such as spider mites, aphids or whiteflies, can be tougher to control and may spread plant diseases. To combat these pests, try products for organic pest control.

Container Plant Watering

When to Water Container Plants

Potted plants tend to dry out more quickly than their in-ground counterparts. The small soil space and the construction of the pot mean the container stores very little moisture. In general, early morning or early evening is the optimal time to water your containers, as this will give the plant some time to take up the water before the heat of the day kicks in, but it will also allow excess water on the plant to evaporate quickly so that the plant is not vulnerable to fungus. It is also obviously time to water when the soil is dry all the way to the bottom, but this may be too late for the plant. Look for shriveled leaves, limp stems, dropping petals, and dry, discolored leaves. You should check potted plants daily in warm, dry conditions. Usually when the first inch (2.5 cm.) or so of soil is dry, it's a good indication that watering is needed. In summer, watering outdoor potted plants is necessary daily (and even twice a day) for most species, especially when temperatures reach over 85 degrees F. (29 C.).

How Often to Water Potted Plants

If you are consistently checking the pots, you will know when to water the plant. The frequency depends upon the species. Succulents and drought tolerant plants need to be watered less often than annuals and vegetables. Well-established plants can go longer before water than newly installed plants. It is best on most plants to water deeply and slowly, so water can access all parts of the soil and roots. Short, light watering just goes out the drainage holes before the plant can acquire the moisture or the soil can absorb the water. In fact, most potting soils can start to repel water if allowed to completely dry out. Slow and deep watering will not only ensure the water gets to the roots of the plant, but will also force over dry potting soil to absorb water again.

If you have accidentally allowed the soil in your container to dry out completely, it would be wise to soak the entire container in a tub of water for a half hour or so in order to force rehydration of the potting soil. Container plant watering on baskets and coir or moss lined wire cages works best if you dunk the entire container in a bucket of water and let it soak.

How Much Water for Container Plants

The amount of water may vary from species to species. Find out the average moisture needs of your particular plant and then get a moisture gauge. These are very useful tools for container plant watering. The gauge has a probe that you stick into the soil and gives you a reading that rates the soil moisture level. If your plant needs moderately moist soil and the gauge reads in the drier zones, it is time to water. If you practice slow deep irrigation, water until the moisture leaches from the drainage holes. Let the top few inches (5 to 10 cm.) of soil dry out before watering again. Knowing how much water for container plants is appropriate is usually a matter of trial and error until you know your particular plant's preferences.

Tips for Watering Outdoor Potted Plants

Container plants outdoors need more water than those indoors. This is because higher temperatures, direct sunlight, and wind, dry the soil quickly. These tips will make watering your potted plants easier:

- Use glazed pots to help prevent evaporation or place clay pots in another container.
- Apply a layer of mulch or rocks to the soil surface to slow moisture loss.
- Set up a drip irrigation system for watering outdoor potted plants. This allows for slow, even watering that the soil can absorb before it all runs through the pot and out the drainage holes.

- Apply water in early morning or late evening when temperatures are cooler and direct sun will not cook off the moisture before it can seep down to the roots.

Conclusion

Container gardening is a popular way to grow various plants without sacrificing valuable space in your backyard. It's a great place to start if you're new to the hobby, as you can control the variables much easier than starting from the ground.